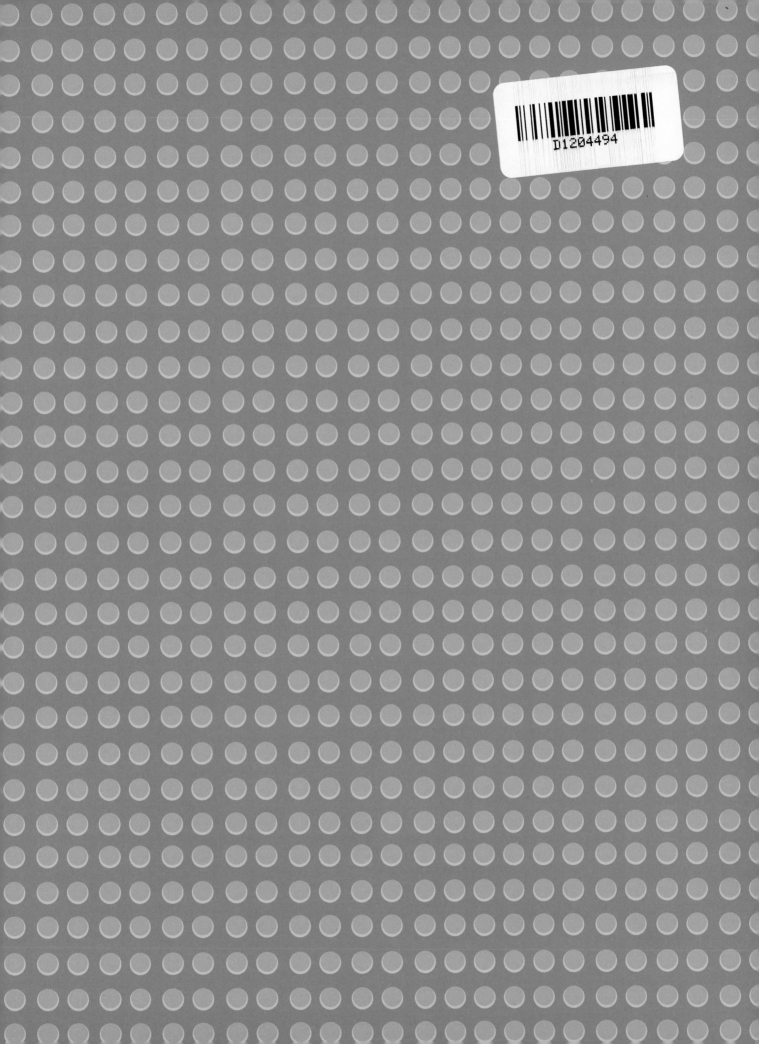

BRICK
BUILDING 101

by Courtney Sanchez
with Jessica Wright
Illustrated by Natasha Hellegouarch

Brimming with creative inspiration, how-to projects, and useful information to enrich your everyday life, Quarto Knows is a favorite destination for those pursuing their interests and passions. Visit our site and dig deeper with our books into your area of interest: Quarto Creates, Quarto Cooks, Quarto Homes, Quarto Lives, Quarto Drives, Quarto Explores, Quarto Gifts, or Quarto Kids.

© 2018 Quarto Publishing Group USA Inc.
Text and photographs © 2018 Courtney Sanchez

First Published in 2018 by Walter Foster Jr., an imprint of The Quarto Group.
6 Orchard Road, Suite 100, Lake Forest, CA 92630, USA.
T (949) 380-7510 **F** (949) 380-7575 **www.QuartoKnows.com**

Walter Foster Jr. titles are also available at discount for retail, wholesale, promotional, and bulk purchase. For details, contact the Special Sales Manager by email at specialsales@quarto.com or by mail at The Quarto Group, Attn: Special Sales Manager, 401 Second Avenue North, Suite 310, Minneapolis, MN 55401 USA.

LEGO®, the LEGO logo, the Brick and Knob configurations, and the Minifigure® are trademarks of the LEGO Group, which does not sponsor, authorize or endorse this book.

ISBN: 978-1-63322-522-0

Digital edition published in 2018
eISBN: 978-1-63322-523-7

Curriculum consulting by Jessica Wright
Illustrated by Natasha Hellegouarch

Printed in China
10 9 8 7 6 5 4 3 2 1

Table of Contents

Introduction

What is STEAM?

The acronym STEAM stands for **Science**, **Technology**, **Engineering**, **Art**, and **Math**. STEAM learning is about giving children real-life problem-solving skills through exploration, play, and exciting learning experiences. STEAM engages kids to find their own solutions. Instead of hearing or reading about gravity and force, STEAM kids build egg-drop contraptions and let them fall. If the egg cracks, they try again. Kids learn by doing, failing, and trying again. That's STEAM!

How to Use This Book

The twenty STEAM activities in this book focus on using LEGO® bricks (big and small), baseplates, and Minifigures®, along with other materials you can easily find around the home. From building a balloon-powered race car and a fidget spinner to learning letters, numbers, shapes, and more, these projects will provide hours of open-ended fun, experimentation, and collaboration.

Each project also includes the following sections:
- **Parent Prep:** Provides tips on what adults can do ahead of time to ensure a fun and engaging activity.
- **STEAM Stats:** Includes information on how each project incorporates one or more of the STEAM categories.
- **STEAM Sparks:** Gives advanced engineers more ideas and new challenges for extending the project.

Every kid is already a budding engineer, especially when it comes to playing with LEGO® bricks. These projects build on that natural enthusiasm in new and exciting ways, making learning fun and rewarding for kids and enjoyable for parents and teachers!

Parents: Look for this symbol.

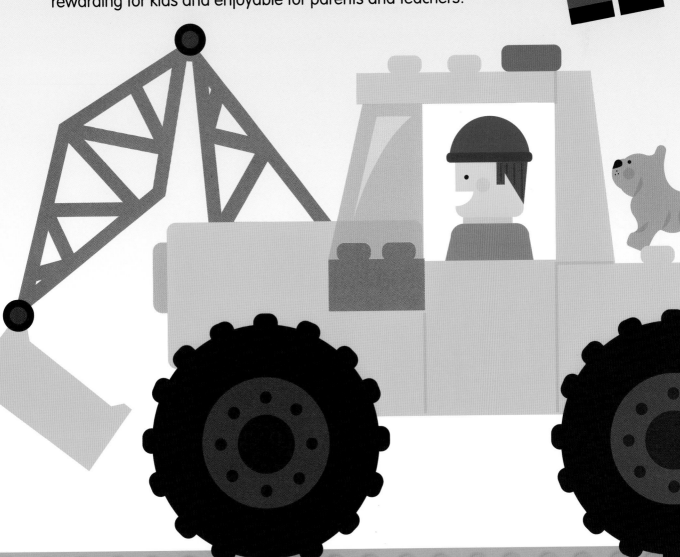

EASY

B is for Build It!

LEGO® bricks make perfect block letters!

You can build all of the letters of the alphabet with LEGO® bricks.

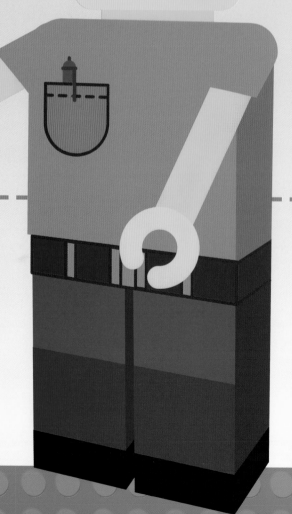

Materials

ABCDE
FGHIJ
KLMNO
PQRSTU
VWXYZ

Bricks   +   Chart on page 9

Parent Prep

Your child might need help figuring out how to use the letter chart on page 9. Show your child which blocks go with the ones in the diagrams, and perhaps build a few letters with your child at first.

Start with the letter A. Look at the letter chart and gather the blocks you need to build it.

Place the blocks on a table and put them together in the shape of an A.

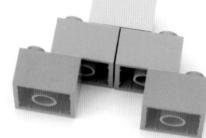

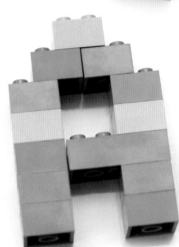

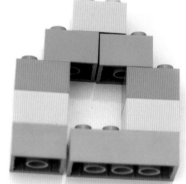

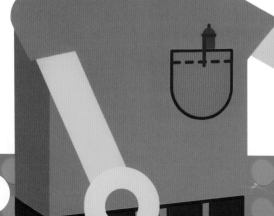

I can spell my name with **LEGO**® bricks. Can you?

Letter Chart

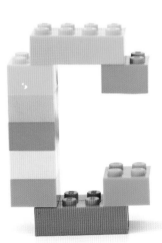

Building letters with bricks will quickly help your child learn to identify the alphabet and early sight words. This activity is also great for building engineering and art skills by having the kids build the letters themselves.

STEAM Sparks

★ How many words can you spell with your letters?

★ Can you spell the word "red" with only red bricks or the word "blue" with only blue bricks?

★ Try building your name with giant letters!

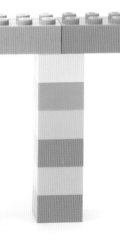

3 When you have finished the letter A, try the others.

Geoboard

Use your LEGO® baseplates to make super cool shapes!

Geoboards are one of my favorite activities! We can have fun learning numbers, letters, and even shapes. So let's give those bands a stretch and get started!

Materials

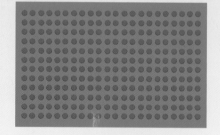

Loom bands   +   **Baseplate**

Parent Prep

Purchase loom bands online or at craft stores in the jewelry section. When first introducing geoboards, create the shapes, numbers, or letters first, and then have your child place bands over yours.

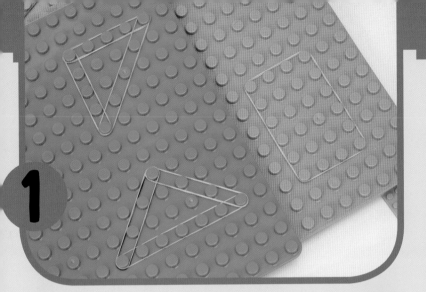

1

Let's begin by making shapes. What shapes can you make?

2

Next, try making numbers and letters.

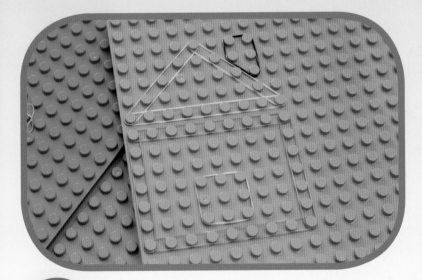

3 What other objects can you make using geoboards? How about a house?

STEAM Stats

Geoboards help develop early mathematical skills as well as shape recognition and concepts of symmetry, while giving children experience with problem solving, critical thinking, and fine-motor skills.

STEAM Sparks

★ Create your numbers and shapes using the chart on page 80!

EASY

Stamp & Squish

Write your ABC's with LEGO® bricks and dough!

Here you can learn your letters using both of my favorite toys! I can't wait.

Materials

Bricks + **Kid-safe modeling compound or dough**

Rolling pin

Parent Prep

Write the letters on a piece of paper for your children so they can recreate them with bricks and dough. For even more fun, create a little spinner (see image on the right) that they can use to decide which letter they should stamp and squish next.

1

Make your dough as flat as a pancake!

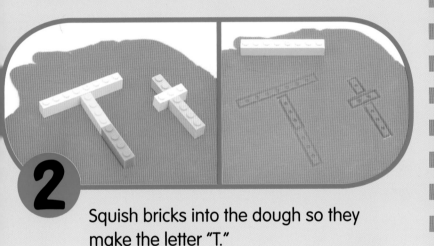

2

Squish bricks into the dough so they make the letter "T."

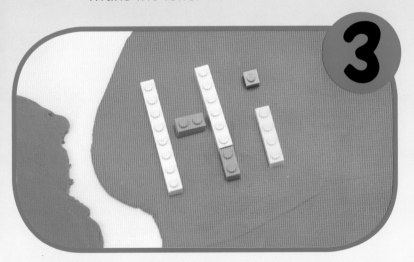

3

What words can you spell? Try spelling "HI," "MOM," and "FUN."

STEAM Stats

This project is perfect for developing fine-motor skills and problem solving abilities while also working on letter recognition and creativity. Budding engineers will be fascinated with the spinner.

STEAM Sparks

★ Dip bricks into paint and press them onto paper.

★ Make your own dough with 1 cup (120 g) flour, ½ cup (118 ml) warm water, ¼ cup (68 ml) salt, and 3 drops natural food coloring.

EASY

Tic-Tac-Toe

Play a fun game with your LEGO® bricks.

The goal of tic-tac-toe is to get three of your pieces in a row. A row can go across, up and down, or diagonally.

Materials

   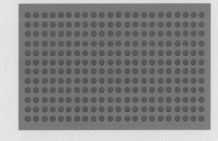

Square bricks   +   **Long and narrow bricks**   +   **Baseplate**

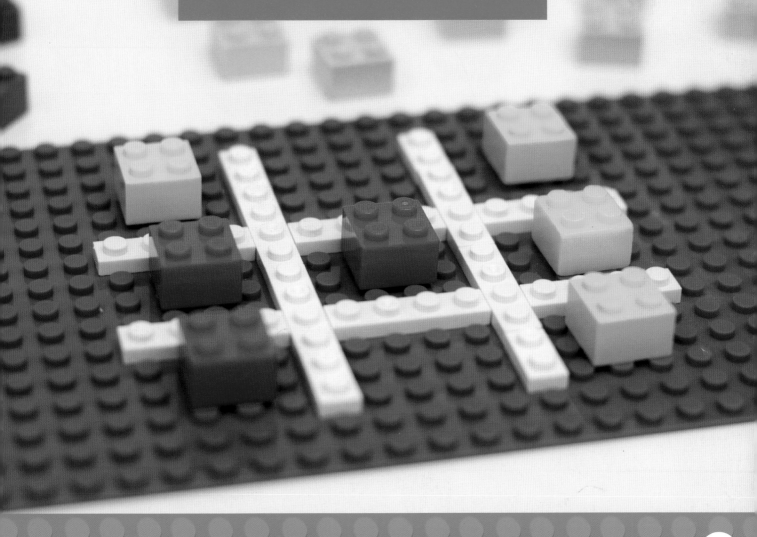

Parent Prep

Your child may need some help designing the game board. Encourage them to experiment and to keep trying, but also be ready to help if frustration sets in.

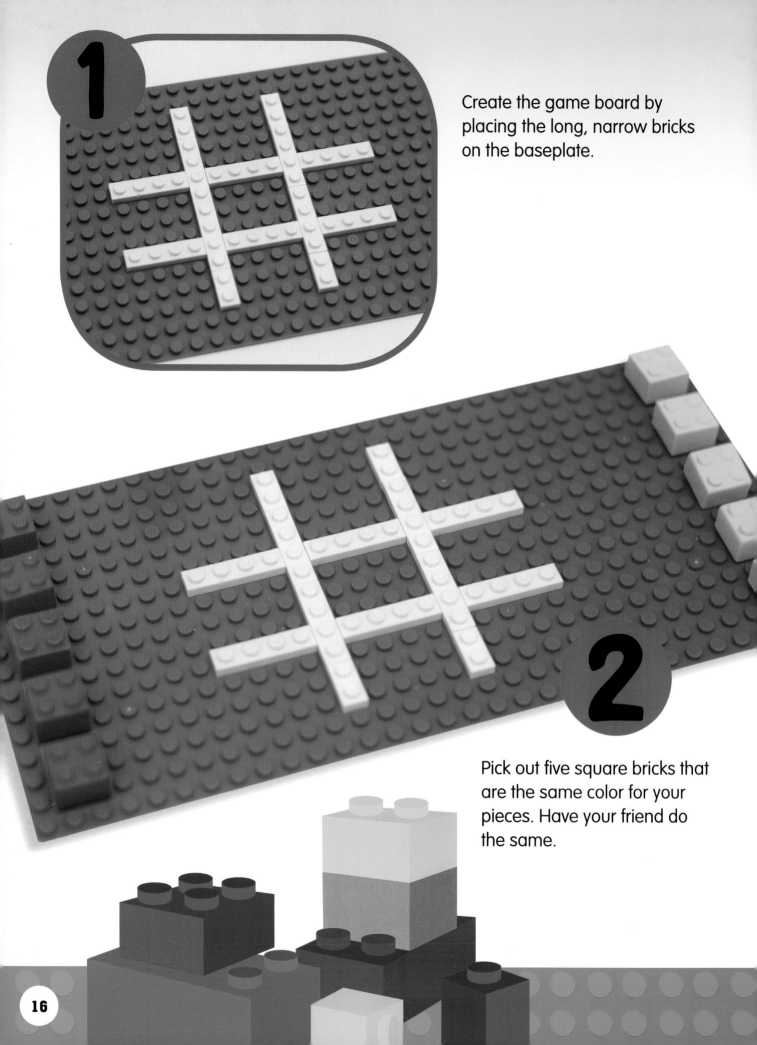

1 Create the game board by placing the long, narrow bricks on the baseplate.

2 Pick out five square bricks that are the same color for your pieces. Have your friend do the same.

STEAM Stats

Children will use their fine-motor skills as well as math and engineering knowledge to build their own game board. Even simple games such as tic-tac-toe will do wonders to boost your child's strategic thinking skills.

3

Take turns placing one brick at a time on the game board. Whoever gets three of their bricks in a row first wins! If the game ends and no one has gotten three bricks in a row, it's a tie!

STEAM Sparks

★ This is a fun game to take on long car rides, trips, and play dates.

★ Create a game board so you can play four-in-a-row tic-tac-toe!

★ Instead of choosing the same color bricks for your pieces, try using the same size bricks instead.

Look! Yellow wins!

EASY

Memory Game

Put your brain to the test!

How good are you at remembering things? I bet you're awesome! This game is like playing Concentration, but you get to build fun objects first!

Materials

Bricks

12 matching paper cups

Parent Prep

Build six fun objects and have your little engineers build the matching pieces. Once they get the hang of the game, they can probably do both steps themselves.

1 Your adult built six fantastic objects. Can you build six matching designs?

2

Place a cup over each object. Mix the cups around and no peeking!

You need twelve cups to play this game. Can you count the cups all by yourself?

3

To play the game, look under two cups. If the items underneath match, you get to keep them. If not, put the items back under the cup and try again. Play until you find all six pairs.

Oh, well.
Try again!

Playing this game helps children develop focus, memory, and recognition skills. Creating a pattern and building the matching pieces before playing also teaches math building concepts.

STEAM Sparks

★ Design and build all of the matching objects yourself!

★ Add more objects (and cups!) to the game.

EASY

Shadow
Monsters

Create cool creatures with LEGO® bricks.

Are you ready to make some super-silly monsters? I sure am! We're going to need a BIG helper for this activity: the sun!

Materials

Bricks + Paper + Markers or crayons + Sunlight

Parent Prep

Test out the best time and place for this activity before you get started. Early mornings and late afternoons are great times for long shadows. Another option is to use a flashlight on a not-so-sunny day.

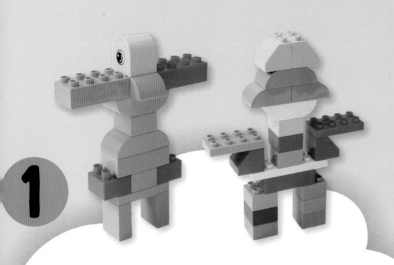

1

Build a LEGO® monster! There's no wrong way to build one! I bet yours is scary.

2

Place your monster in a sunny location. Put a piece of paper where its shadow is, and trace the shadow.

Design your shadow monster.

3

STEAM Stats

This shadow art project is a great STEAM activity that will get your preschooler's creative juices flowing! It's also a fun way to incorporate engineering (building) and science (experimenting) into a drawing activity.

STEAM Sparks

★ Take the super silly monsters outside and draw shadows with chalk.

★ Keep your monster in the same place, but trace it at different times during the day. What is happening with its shadow?

★ Why do shadows change throughout the day?

EASY

The Slime Game

Here's a gooey game you'll have some sticky fun with.

Your LEGO® Minifigures® are going to love swimming in slime!

Materials

½ cup (125 ml) white glue

+

1½ cups (340 g) shaving cream

2½ tablespoons contact saline solution

+

Food coloring

Parent Prep

Measure out the ingredients for the slime ahead of time, but let your child add and mix them. Don't forget to let them help with the clean-up after the fun!

Mini foam balls (optional)

Measuring cups & spoons

1

Measure out all of the slime ingredients and mix them up in a bowl.

Grab your Minifigures® and separate them into tops and bottoms. Mix them up and stick them in the slime.

2

Ewww!

3

Dig through the slime and match the tops and bottoms of your figures.

When you're done with your gooey game, place your slimed figures in a bowl of hot water, and the slime will come right off!

STEAM Stats

The science of slime will fascinate kids of all ages. Not only will this gooey game help with fine-motor skills while creating a challenging game of "match 'em," but children will also experience the thrill of mixing ingredients to create something new…and squishy!

STEAM Sparks

★ With an adult's help, use different portions of the slime ingredients. How does the slime change?

★ This is a great time to learn about measuring cups and spoons and how they are used in cooking.

Know Your Numbers

Are you ready to practice your numbers with this fun game?

I'm counting on it! All you have to do is roll the dice and find the number on your game board! Easy peasy!

Materials

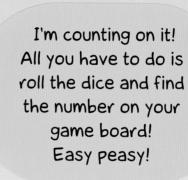

Square bricks + **2 Dice**

Paper + **Markers**

Parent Prep

Write the numbers 1 through 12 on a
sheet of paper as shown.

1

Roll the dice.

2

Count the little black dots. Did you roll a five? Find that number on your game board and place FIVE bricks on top of that number! Good job!

Count your blocks out loud. This is a great way to help you remember your numbers and practice counting!

STEAM Stats

This game introduces important concepts, such as learning to count, identifying numbers, and understanding quantity.

STEAM Sparks

★ Create a new game board with the numbers 1 through 18, and add a third dice to roll!

★ How many bricks can you stack before they topple over?

3 Keep rolling the dice until you have covered up the numbers 1 through 12!

Super Symmetry

Create a mirror image!

Symmetry means that two sides of an object or a picture are the same. Learn more about symmetry with this really fun project!

Materials

Bricks + **Baseplate**

Parent Prep

Create a dividing line down the middle of the baseplate with long, thin bricks so your child can easily tell the difference between the two sides of the project. Using a variety of bricks, make a simple, colorful design on one side of the divider. Also, set aside the exact pieces needed so your preschooler can enjoy early success with recreating the design.

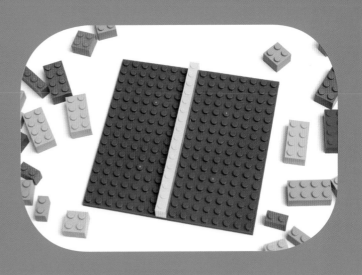

1 Look at the design closely that a parent made for you.

2 Copy the design on the other side with your bricks.

You're doing a great job!

3

You did it!

What in nature is symmetrical? A butterfly? A face? A ladybug? Look around and find symmetrical objects.

Simple geometric shapes are often symmetrical. Symmetry is an important concept when drawing and working with shapes.

STEAM Sparks

★ Have an adult create one-half of this ladybug design. Can you create the other half?

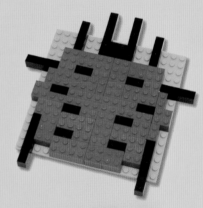

MODERATE

Zippy Zip Line

Send your LEGO® Minifigures® on a zippy adventure!

This is a perfect project for some really creative building. Get ready to slip, zip, and slide!

Materials

Bricks   +   Minifigures®   +   Rope

Parent Prep

Suggest a couple of locations for the rope ends and tie the rope once you child has chosen spots. Guide your child as needed in creating a zip-line-worthy carrier.

1

Build a carrier for your Minifigure®. Make sure there's room for the rope at the top!

2

Tie one end of the rope to the back of a chair. Thread the rope through the top of the zip-line carrier you built. Tie the other end of the rope to the leg of a table.

Make sure one end of the rope is higher than the other.

3 Bring the carrier to the high end of the rope and then let it go! Zoom!

STEAM Stats

Young builders will enjoy designing and experimenting with the carrier as well as with where to put the rope. This is a great time to talk about how gravity works.

STEAM Sparks

★ How can you fix the rope so the zip-line carrier will move faster?

★ What are other ways to make your zip line zippier?

Pretty Planter

Watch a seed grow into a plant!

> Do you know how plants grow? Well, we're going to find out by building our very own planter and waiting for a seed grow into a plant!

Materials

Bricks + **Baseplate**

Coffee filters + **Sunflower or other type of seed**

Small rocks + **Potting soil** + **Water**

Parent Prep

When choosing a seed to grow, try sunflower, grass, herbs, or lima beans. Also, when creating the planter, show your child how to build a box so it won't fall apart or leak.

Create a square or rectangular box. Make the walls of your planter 6 bricks high so your plant has room to grow.

When laying bricks on top of your previous layer, make sure one brick sits on top of two bricks. This makes your wall nice and strong!

Add two coffee filters to the bottom of the planter. This helps keep the dirt and water in the planter. Next, add in some rocks.

2

3

Add the dirt. Push it into the planter. Add the seed and give it some water.

Your plant will need plenty of air, water, and sunlight to grow!

STEAM Stats

Planting seeds in a homemade planter is a great science and engineering activity. Kids will quickly learn whether or not their planter has been engineered so it can hold dirt and water.

STEAM Sparks

★ When your seedling gets too big for its planter, transplant it to the yard or a bigger planter. You will be amazed to see changes in your growing plant.

★ Make more than one planter and grow different seeds in each. Which seeds grow the fastest?

Marvelous Marble Maze

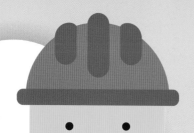

Do you like mazes? Here's one you can build yourself.

There's no doubt about it: you're going to roll for this easy-to-make marble maze runner.

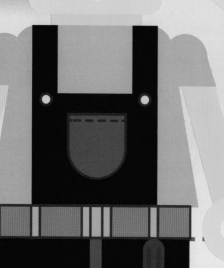

Materials

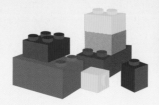

Bricks   +   Baseplate   +   Marble

Parent Prep

Create your own maze runner while your child works on hers so she can learn from your brick placements. Then, race your marbles to the finish line!

1

Build a brick wall around the edge of the baseplate.

You can use one color for your wall or mix them up!

2

Use long, narrow bricks to fill in the maze.

Don't forget to leave enough room for the marble to go through each spot.

STEAM Stats

Marble runs are classic physics activities that show energy, force, and friction in action, while testing and making design changes to the maze are great engineering activities.

STEAM Sparks

★ When the maze gets too easy, add extra bricks and dead ends, like we did below.

3 To play, place a marble at one end and tilt the maze to guide the marble through to the other end.

Build a launching site for your marble in one of the corners.

MODERATE

Fidget Spinner

You'll absolutely spin over this project!

Do you like fidget spinners? I use one all the time! We're going to build a fidget spinner using LEGO® bricks!

Materials

4 Long bricks   +

1 Axle   +

2 Round plates   +   2 Round bricks

 # Parent Prep

Make sure you have the pieces needed on hand before beginning this project. This is one engineering challenge that needs specific pieces to work properly.

 Once you have your pieces, you're ready to build your spinner. Follow the steps shown here.

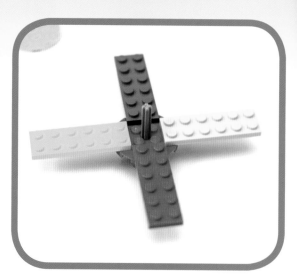

2 Nice work! Now, give it a spin!

 Once you've mastered making this spinner, try creating your own design.

This is a great way for increasing your child's ability to design, plan, and build. There are so many great learning and engineering possibilities with this activity. It also helps with fine-motor skills as well!

STEAM Sparks

★ If you add more weight, does it spin faster or slower?

★ Make a couple of fidget spinners and see which one is the fastest.

MODERATE

Float Your Boat

This project is sure to make a splash!

We're going to test which rafts sink or float when you add pennies and other weights to them.

Materials

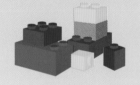

Bricks + **Pennies**

Water + **Straws (optional)** + **Kid-safe modeling compound (optional)**

Foam sheet (optional)

Parent Prep

Give your child the freedom to experiment and create whatever raft he or she wishes. Ask guiding questions such as, "Why do you think this raft will hold a lot of weight?"

1 Build a flat bottom for your raft. Then build up the sides. Be as creative as you want!

2 Once your raft is done, make a few more!

3 Are you ready to test these rafts out in the water? Let's do it!

How many pennies can your rafts hold before they flip over and sink? Which one can hold the most pennies?

This activity is a great opportunity for preschoolers to test out their engineering and science skills. This is also a perfect way to problem solve and test through trial and error while having some water fun!

STEAM Sparks

★ If you want to take your raft to the next level, add a sail! You need a straw, foam sheet for your sail, and modeling compound!
Try different designs.

CHALLENGING

Build a Bridge

And watch it fall!

*

*

*

Bridges need to be strong so that cars and trucks can travel safely over rivers and other roads! This activity will help you decide which materials make the best bridges.

Materials

Baseplate + **Bricks**

Straws + **Craft sticks** + **Card stock**

Chenille stems + **Minifigures®**

Parent Prep

Ask your budding engineer one or more of the following leading questions:

Before building:
- What materials do you think we should use to build the strongest bridge?
- What materials will not make a good bridge? Why not?
- How long should the bridge be?

After building:
- How can we make the bridge even stronger?
- What is the heaviest item the bridge can hold?

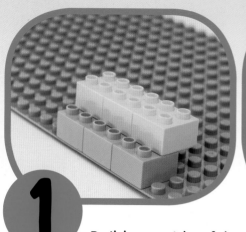 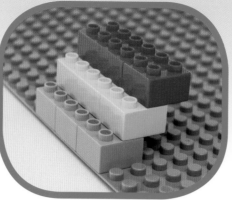 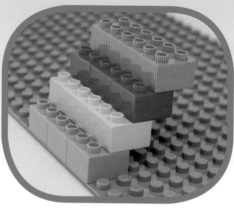

1 Build one side of the bridge with long, rectangular bricks.

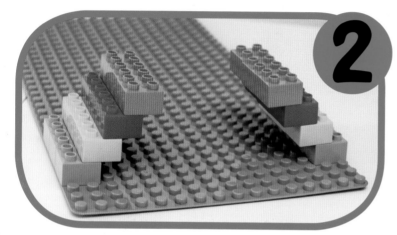

2 Now create the other side of the bridge by copying what you did in step one.

3 Use different materials to create the middle of your bridge.

Place your Minifigures® on the different bridges. Which materials make the strongest bridge?

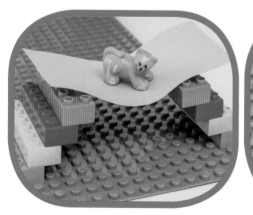 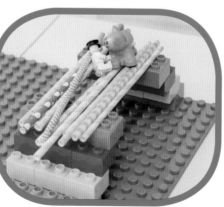 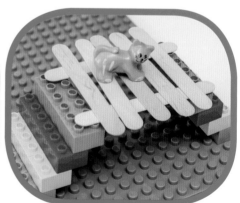

Use bricks to complete the bridge.

4

STEAM Stats

Bridge building is a classic STEAM activity for little engineers. By experimenting with design and process, children learn about how some materials make better bridges than others.

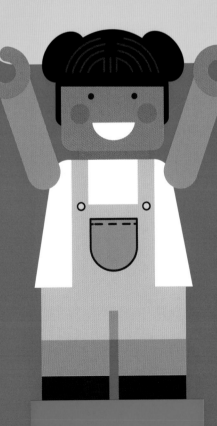

STEAM Sparks

★ Build a city around your bridge.

★ Find other materials to span your bridge.

CHALLENGING

Bird Feeder

This project is for the birds!

This is a great activity for you to use your amazing engineering skills. Do you think you can wing it?

Materials

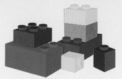

Bricks + **Two 5" x 5" (13 x 13 cm) baseplates**

Birdseed

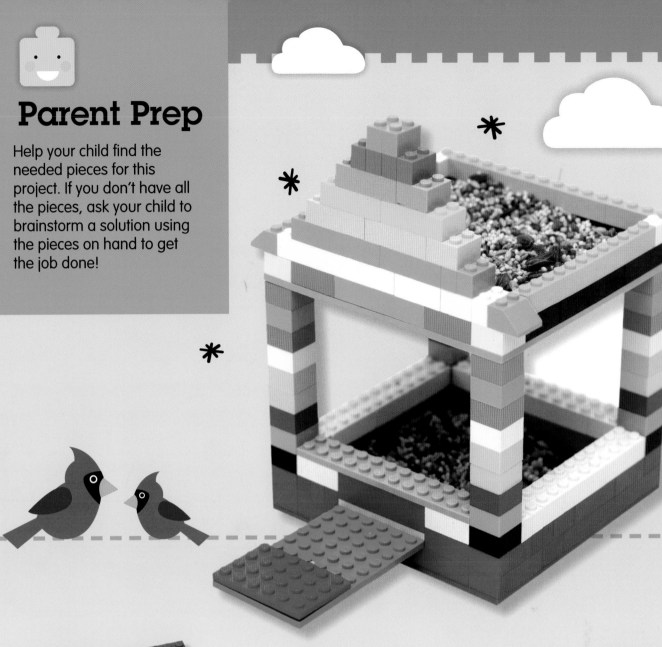

Parent Prep

Help your child find the needed pieces for this project. If you don't have all the pieces, ask your child to brainstorm a solution using the pieces on hand to get the job done!

1 Build a wall around the edge of one baseplate, one row high. Place the perch piece in the middle of one side. Just about any long, thin brick will work.

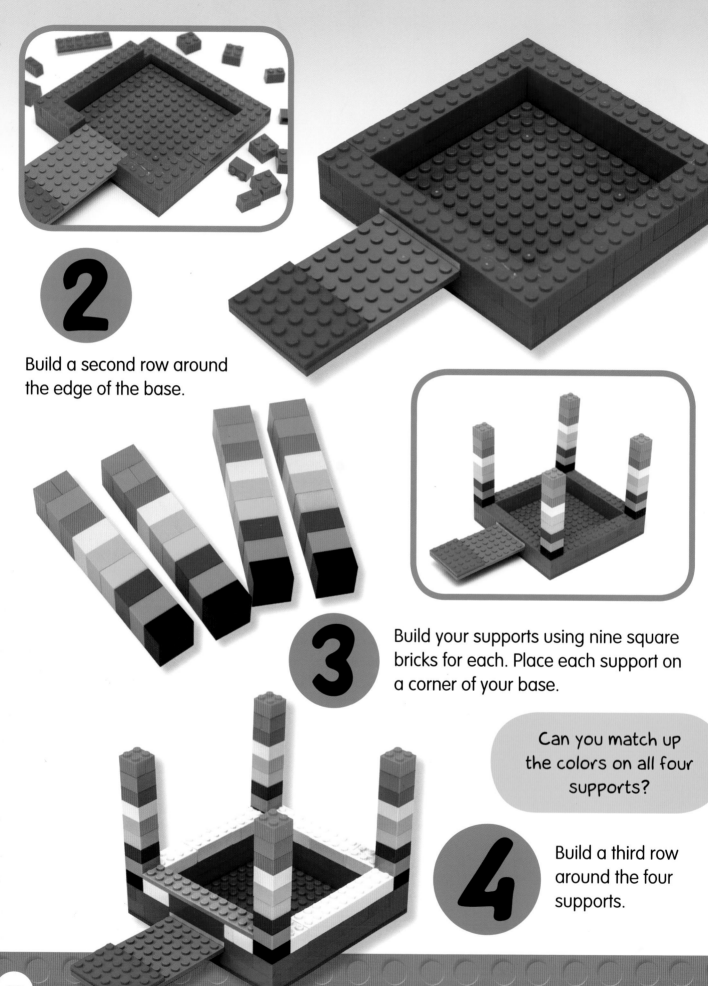

2

Build a second row around the edge of the base.

3

Build your supports using nine square bricks for each. Place each support on a corner of your base.

Can you match up the colors on all four supports?

4

Build a third row around the four supports.

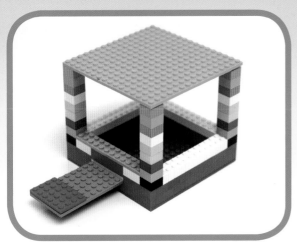

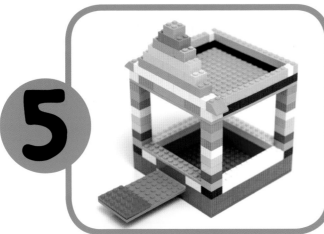

5

Place the second baseplate over the four supports. Then create a fun design!

Add birdseed to the top and bottom of the feeder and head outside!

STEAM Stats

This activity encourages creativity, problem-solving, and engineering skills. Ask your child what would happen if you made the supports taller. How about if you made them shorter?

STEAM Sparks

★ Create a new bird feeder design using your own ideas.

★ Keep track of the types and colors of birds that come to your feeder.

Ready? Set! Launch It!

Send things up, up, up in the air!

A catapult is a contraption that can launch items great distances. Let's build one with bricks and see which items travel the farthest.

Materials

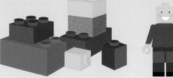

Bricks and Minifigures® +

Wheels

Plastic cup + **Table tennis ball**

Pom-pom ball + **Dice** + **Marshmallows**

Parent Prep

Help your child select the items they can safely launch indoors. Make sure the room is clear of breakable objects, and supervise so your child doesn't take aim at valuables—and siblings!

1 Build your launching pad!

2 Attach a long brick to a pair of wheels. Add a square block to one end of the long brick.

The secret to making the catapult work are the wheels and the long brick.

3 Attach the launching pad to the long brick.

STEAM Stats

Little engineers will love building this simple machine with moving parts. They will also use their math skills while discussing height and distance, as well as their science knowledge while watching gravity and force in action.

STEAM Sparks

★ Build a "well" and practice aiming the catapult so the object will land in it.

★ For your launching items, try different shapes, sizes, and weights. Mark each spot so you can see which items flew the farthest.

4 Launch your items!

CHALLENGING

Balloon Racer

Start your engines!

Attention all racers! Who's ready to build an awesome Balloon Racer? You'll need wheels and axle pieces for this super-fast speedster.

Materials

Bricks, along with wheels + **Balloon**

Axle pieces

Parent Prep

Help your child build the important wheelbase. Then let your budding engineer build whatever on the top. Also, you may need to provide the lung power for the balloon!

1 Create a base for your racer. Add the wheels.

2 Build the back of the car that holds the balloon. Don't leave too much space for the mouth of the balloon, otherwise the balloon will shoot off without the car!

This already looks fast!

3

Blow up the balloon and let your racer go!

STEAM Stats

The science of moving vehicles is fascinating for kids, and they will love experimenting with the balloon engine. Kids will also enjoy experimenting with different designs and seeing which ones go the farthest.

STEAM Sparks

★ Experiment with several different car sizes and shapes and measure to see which car goes the farthest.

★ How high does the back of the car have to be for it to work?

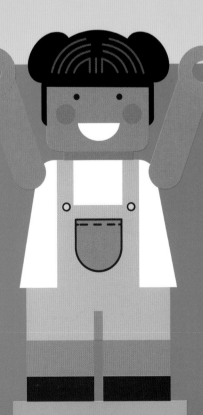

Volcano

Explosive fun awaits!

You'll be bursting with excitement with this project.

Materials

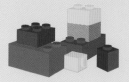

Bricks   +   **Baseplate**

Tall plastic cup   +   **½ cup (115 g) baking soda**   +   **1 cup (250 ml) vinegar**

Food coloring   +   **Dish soap**   +   **Measuring cups**

Parent Prep

This is definitely a project you'll need to stick around for. It's fun, but a tad messy. The volcanic concoction is not toxic, but supervision is recommended, as is some plastic for underneath the volcano. Even better, take it outside!

1

Create the base of your volcano.

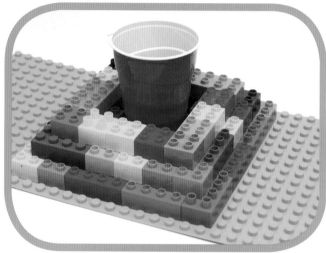

2

Build up the sides of the volcano as shown in the photographs.

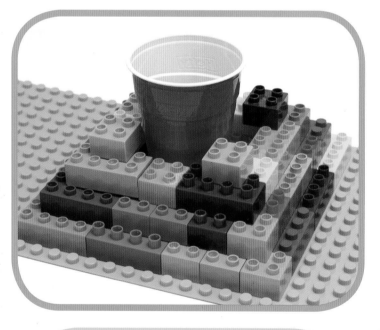

Your volcano will be in the shape of a pyramid—large at the bottom and smaller at the top.

This project introduces the concept of chemistry and chemical reactions to your preschooler in an educational but fun way. This experiment is a perfect way to get your little scientist started out!

STEAM Sparks

★ Experiment with using less or more baking soda or vinegar.

3

To make the lava, follow these steps:

• Pour the baking soda into the cup.

• Squeeze a few drops of dish soap into the baking soda.

• Pour the vinegar into the measuring cup. Add a few drops of food coloring.

• When you're ready to erupt the volcano, pour the vinegar into the cup.

CHALLENGING

The Egg Drop Challenge * *

Get ready for an egg-cellent adventure!

This project will crack you up! Can you build a container that will protect an egg from breaking? Sure you can!

Materials

 Bricks + **Cotton pads** + **Tape** + **Eggs**

 Balloon +  **String** +  **Craft sticks**

 **Chenille stems** +  **Cardboard tube** + **Straws**

Parent Prep

Give your child plenty of room to try different materials and designs.
Provide a wide, outdoor space in which to experiment, and wash the
bricks in hot, soapy water afterward.

1 Make your container bottom and add sides.

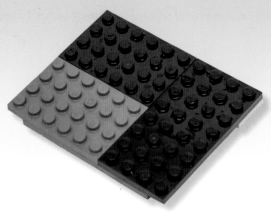

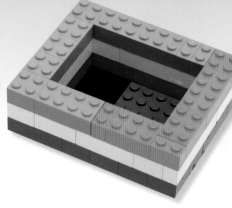

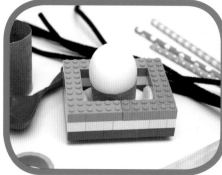

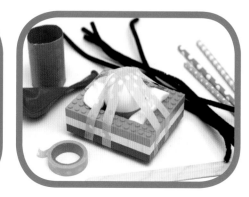

2 Use the materials you've gathered to make your egg safe from breaking.

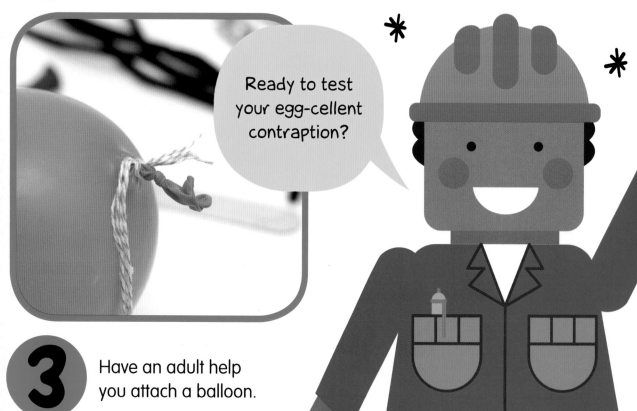

Ready to test your egg-cellent contraption?

3 Have an adult help you attach a balloon.

This activity is all about slowing down gravity and creating a container for the egg that will cushion the fall. Your child will learn about physics while using technology to design a crash-proof egg container.

STEAM Sparks

★ Try designing a parachute to replace the balloon.

★ Once you have a container that saves the egg from cracking, try dropping it from higher up. Get an adult to help.

 4 Find a good spot outside and drop the egg container to the ground. Did your egg survive?

Templates for LEGO® Geoboard Project

About the Author

Courtney Sanchez

A stay-at-home mom of three boys, Courtney Sanchez began crafting as a way to keep her children stimulated and active. Having time to sit and be creative with children, and to explore using texture, colors, and (most importantly) their imaginations, is a great way to bond and teach at the same time. Her website, Crafts by Courtney (www.craftsbycourtney.com), explores a variety of activities and how-to kids' crafts to keep children active and inspired through creative play.